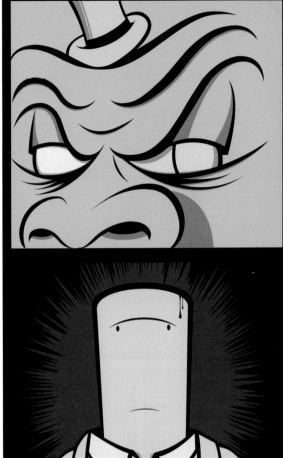

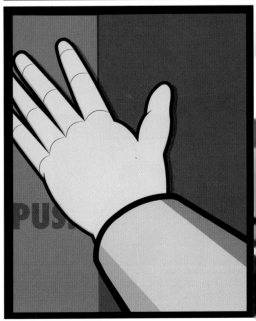

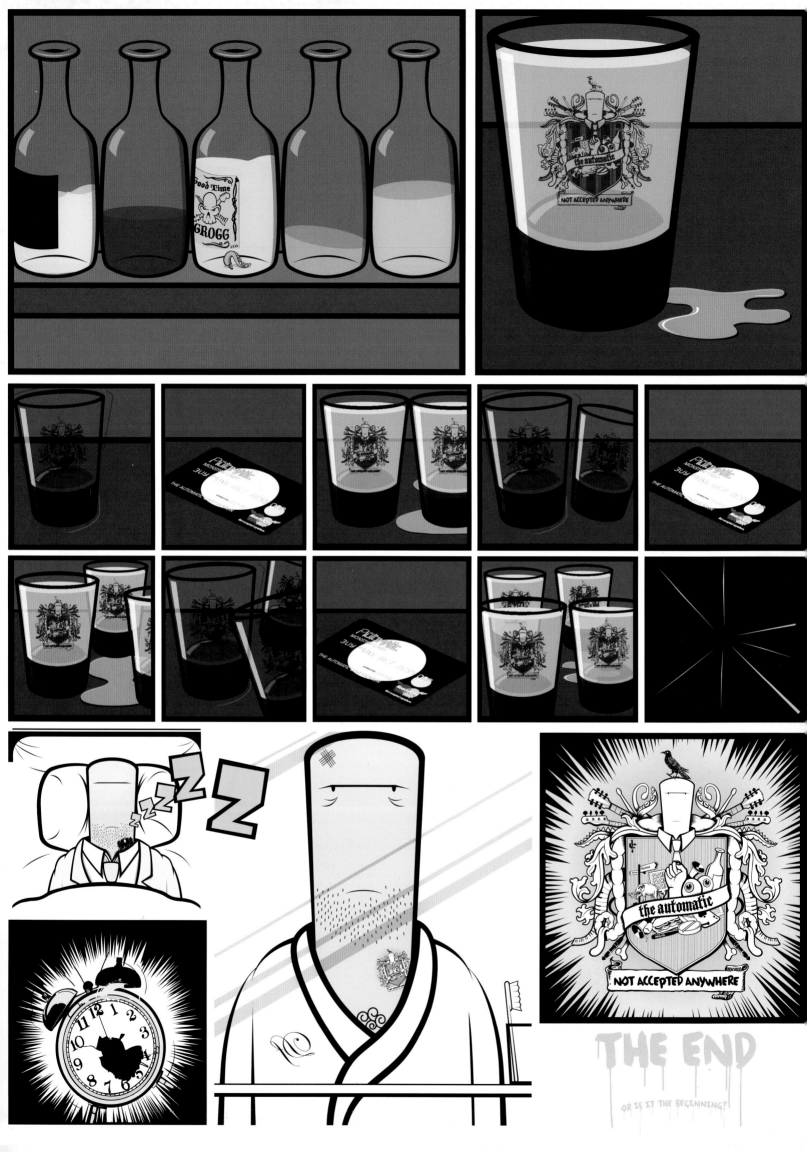

© 2006 BY INTERNATIONAL MUSIC PUBLICATIONS LTD
FIRST PUBLISHED BY INTERNATIONAL MUSIC PUBLICATIONS LTD IN 2006
INTERNATIONAL MUSIC PUBLICATIONS LTD IS A FABER MUSIC COMPANY
3 QUEEN SQUARE, LONDON WC1N 3AU

DESIGNED BY

ARRANGED BY ALEX DAVIS
ENGRAVED BY CAMDEN MUSIC
EDITED BY LUCY HOLLIDAY & OLLY WEEKS

PRINTED IN ENGLAND BY CALIGRAVING LTD
ALL RIGHTS RESERVED

ISBN 0-571-52722-1

TO BUY FABER MUSIC PUBLICATIONS OR TO FIND OUT ABOUT THE FULL RANGE OF TITLES AVAILABLE,
PLEASE CONTACT YOUR LOCAL MUSIC RETAILER OR FABER MUSIC SALES ENQUIRIES:

FABER MUSIC LTD, BURNT MILL, ELIZABETH WAY, HARLOW, CM20 2HX ENGLAND
TEL: +44(0)1279 82 89 82 FAX: +44(0)1279 82 89 83
SALES@FABERMUSIC.COM FABERMUSIC.COM

THAT'S WHAT SHE SAID

WORDS AND MUSIC BY ROBIN HAWKINS, JAMES FROST, IWAN GRIFFITHS AND ALEXANDER PENNIE

1. Pack up your ac - cents, back up your bat - te - ries.
2. So punk is dead and this is so___ new.

(Wow!)

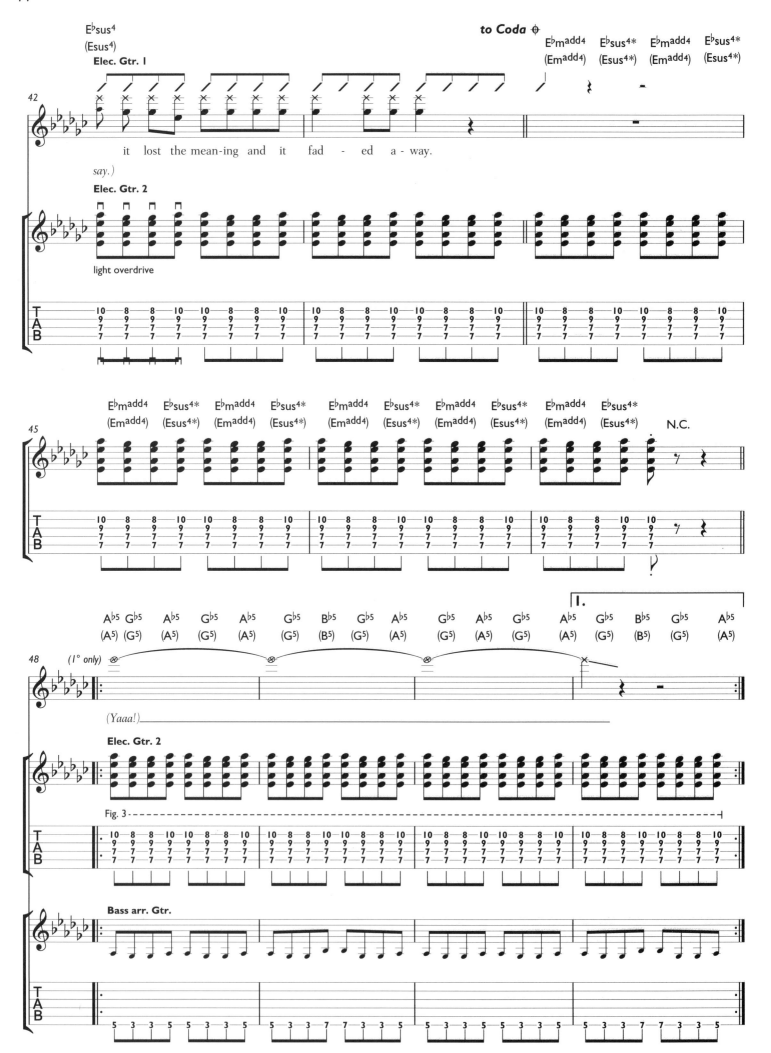

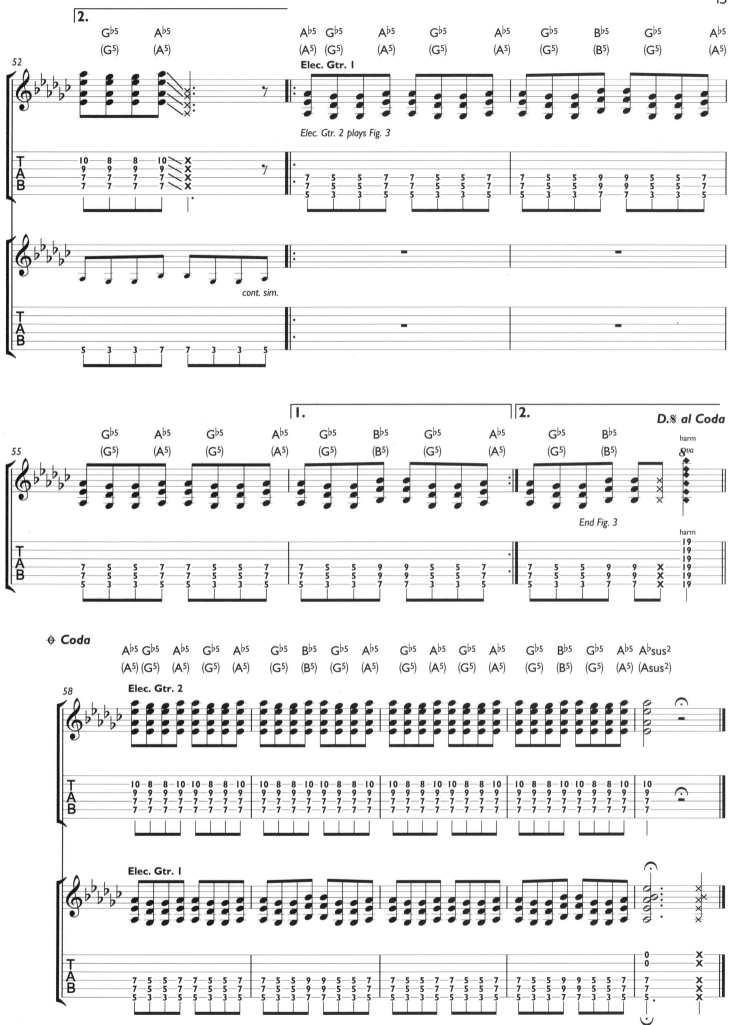

RAOUL

WORDS AND MUSIC BY ROBIN HAWKINS, JAMES FROST, IWAN GRIFFITHS AND ALEXANDER PENNIE

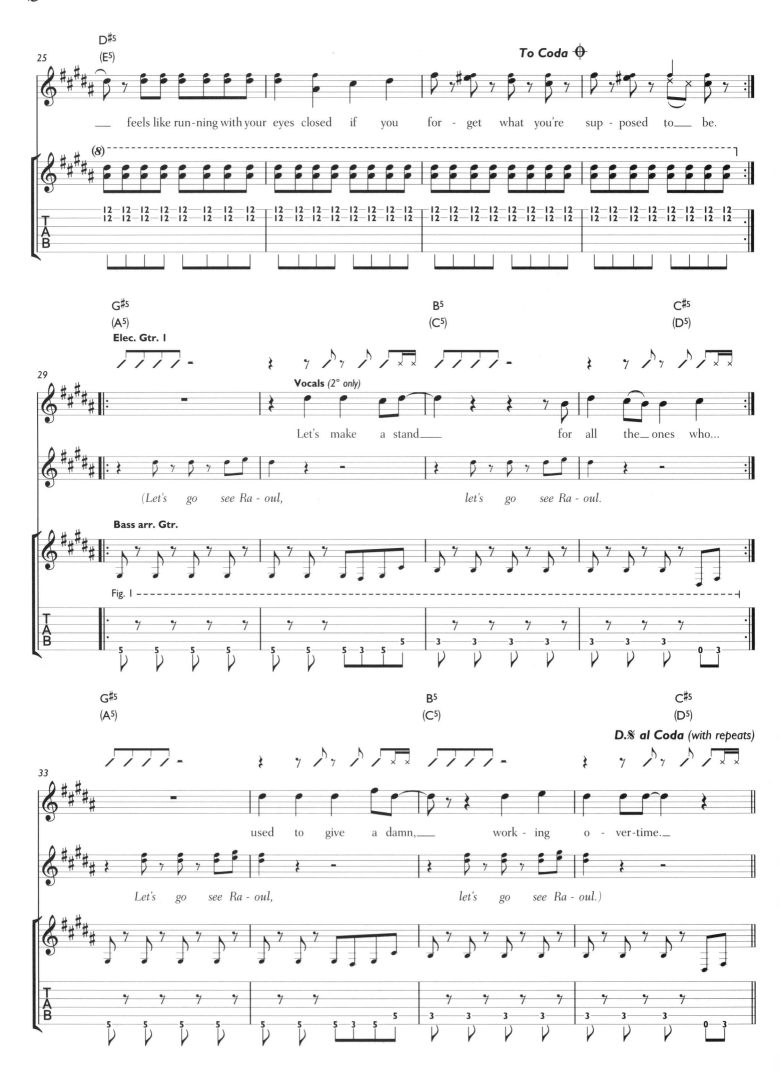

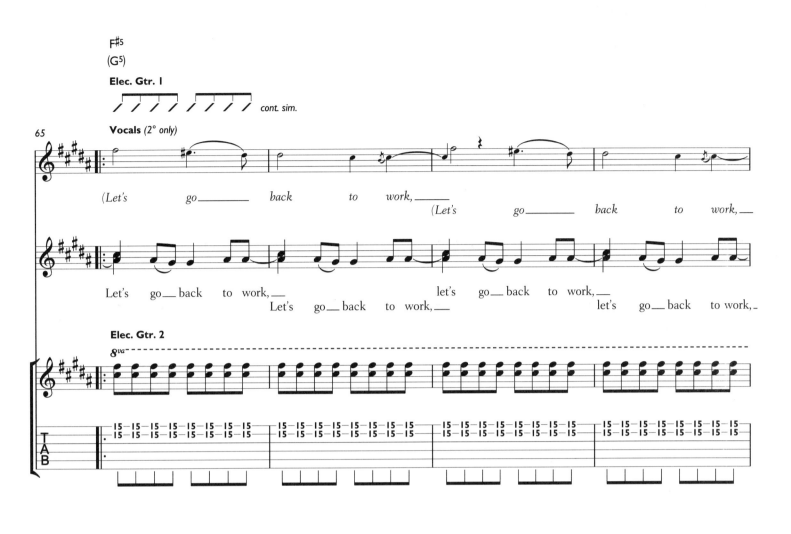

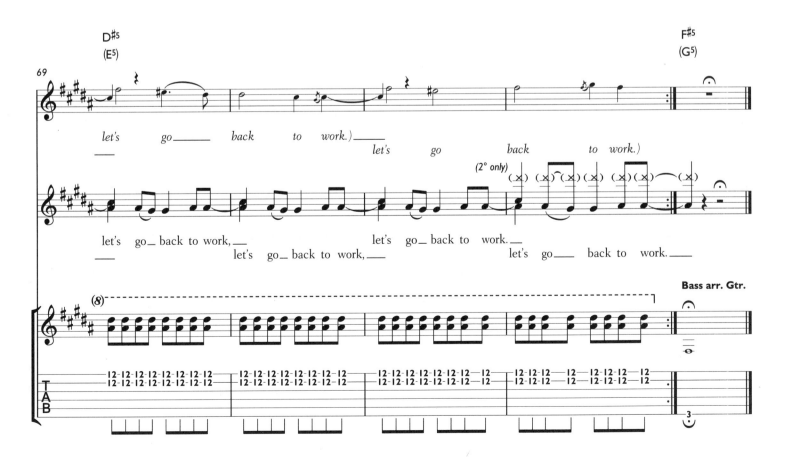

YOU SHOUT YOU SHOUT YOU SHOUT

WORDS AND MUSIC BY ROBIN HAWKINS, JAMES FROST, IWAN GRIFFITHS AND ALEXANDER PENNIE

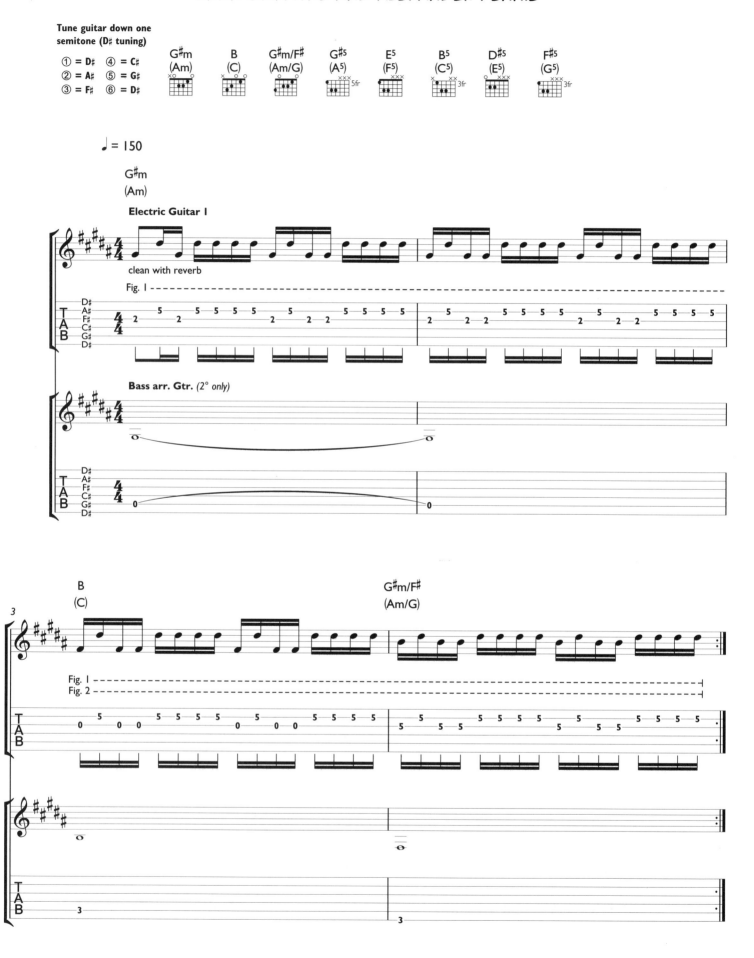

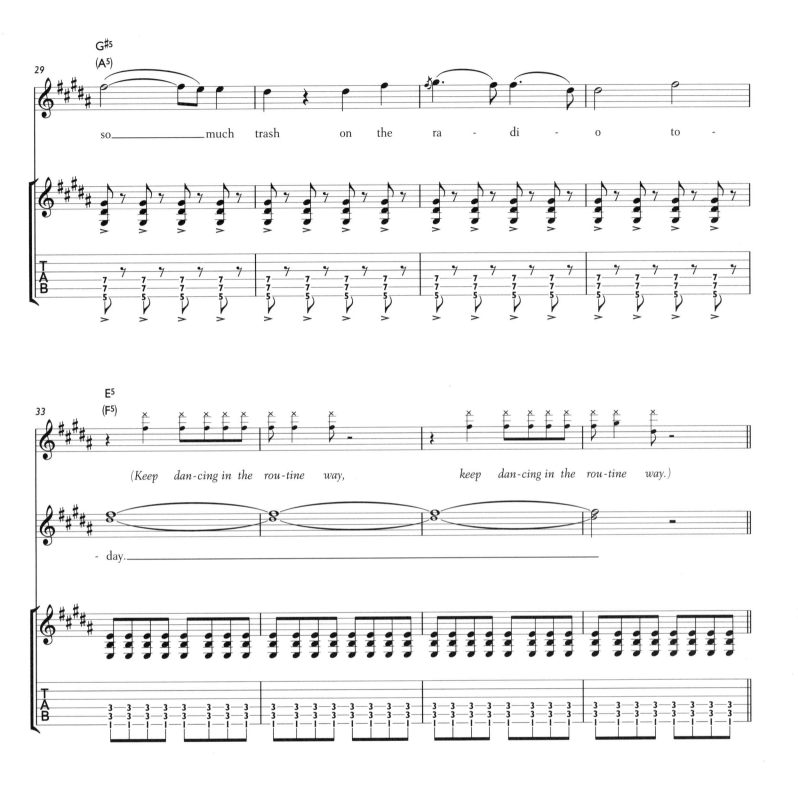

so _____ much trash on the ra - di - o to -

(Keep dan-cing in the rou-tine way,   keep dan-cing in the rou-tine way.)

- day. _____

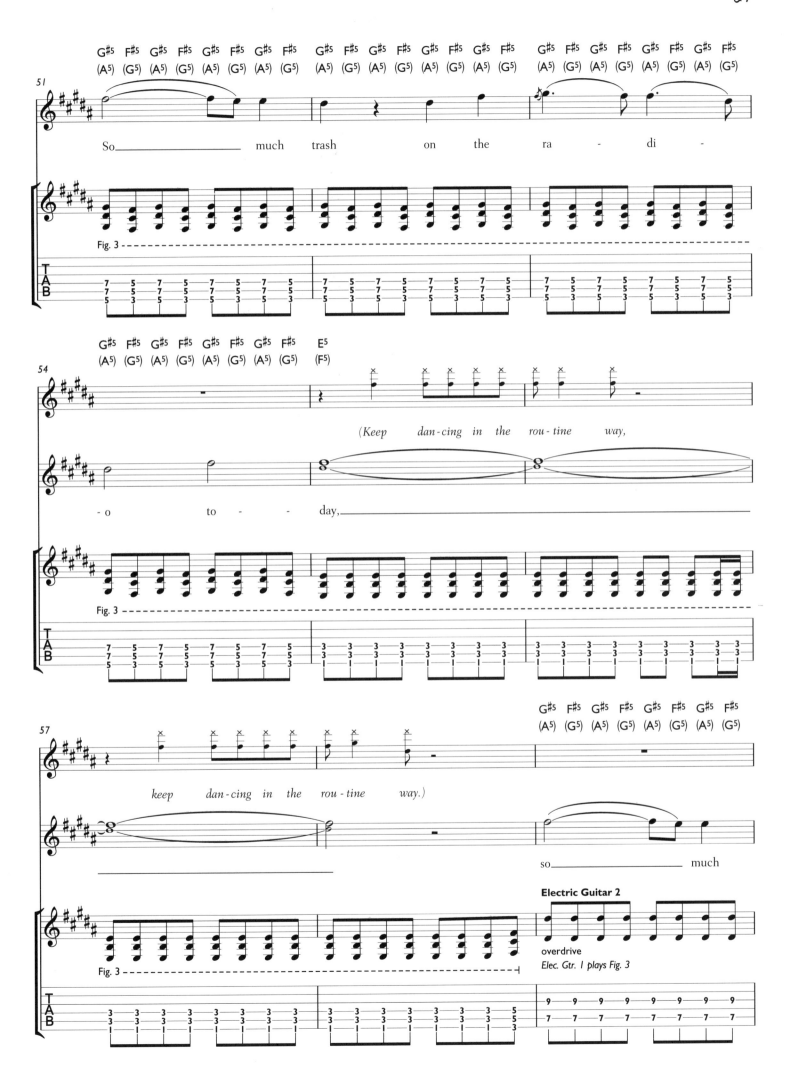

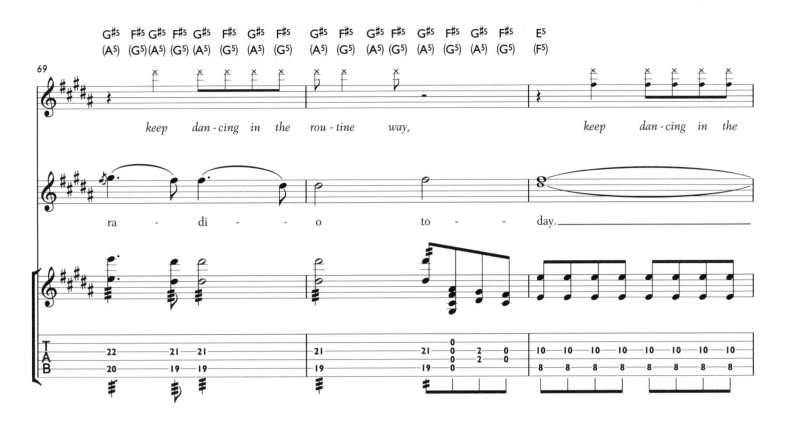

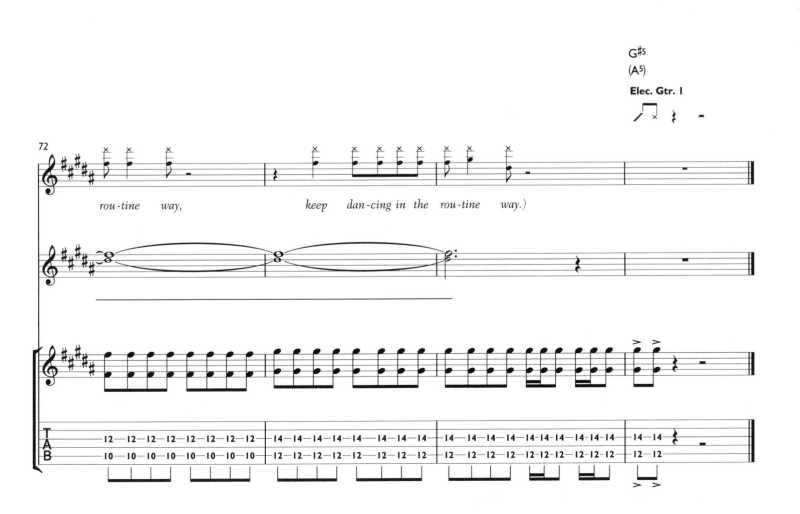

RECOVER

WORDS AND MUSIC BY ROBIN HAWKINS, JAMES FROST, IWAN GRIFFITHS AND ALEXANDER PENNIE

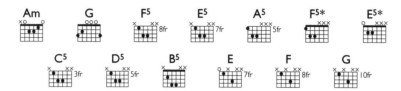

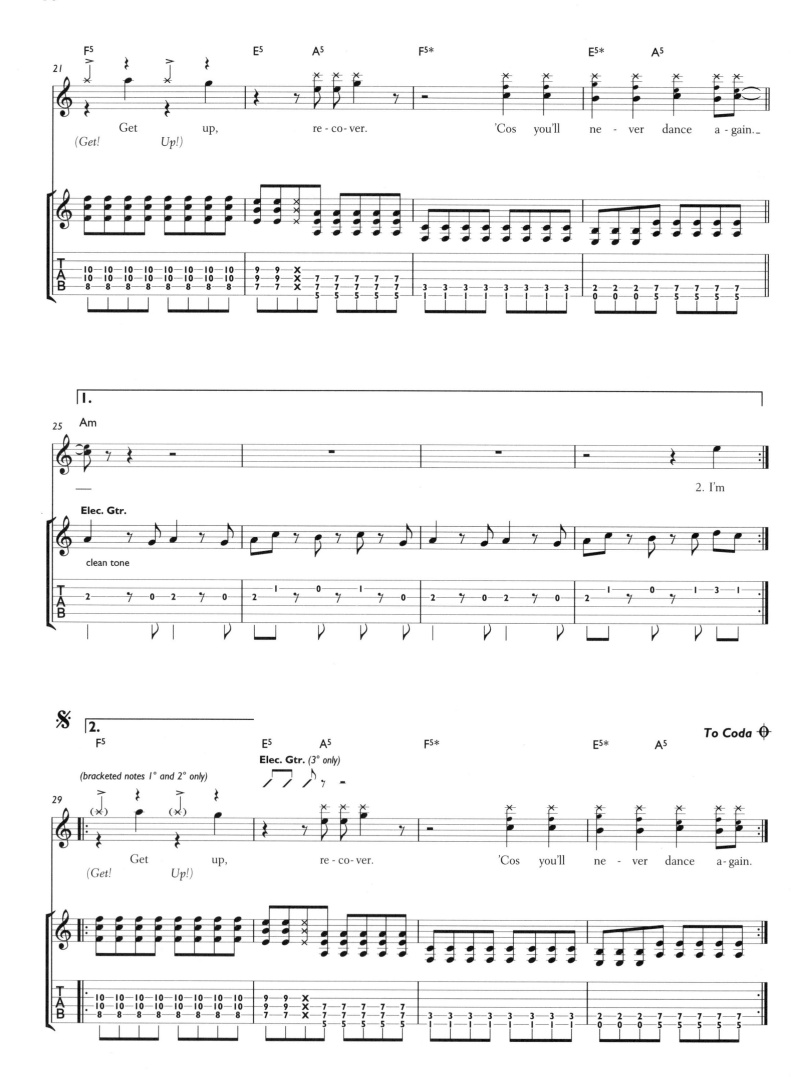

⊕ *Coda*

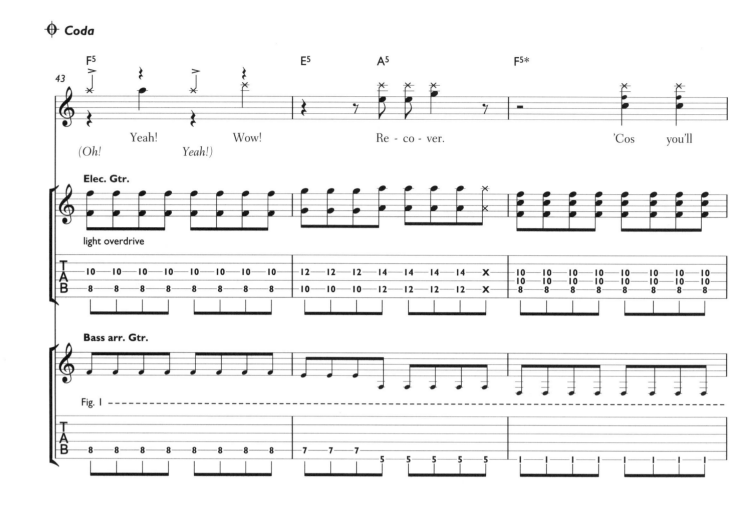

(Oh! — Yeah!) Yeah! — Wow! — Re - co - ver. — 'Cos you'll

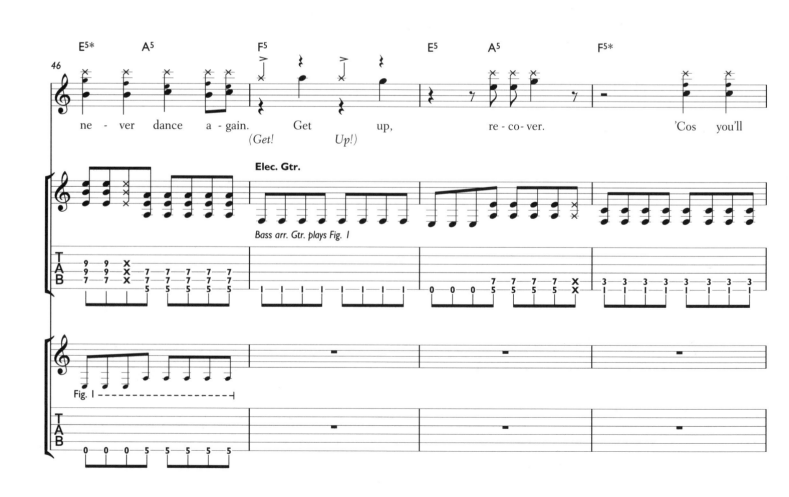

ne - ver dance a - gain. (Get! — Up!) Get up, — re - co - ver. — 'Cos you'll

MONSTER

WORDS AND MUSIC BY ROBIN HAWKINS, JAMES FROST, IWAN GRIFFITHS AND ALEXANDER PENNIE

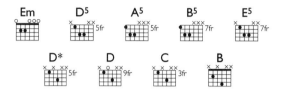

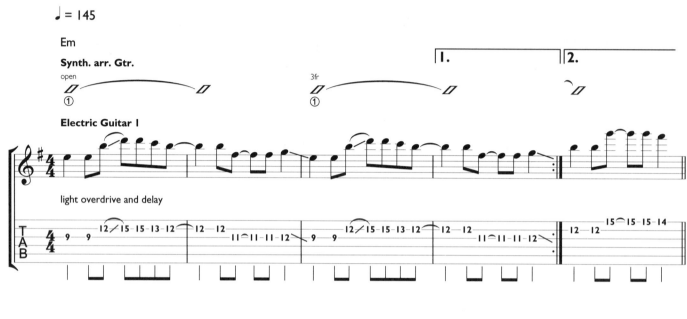

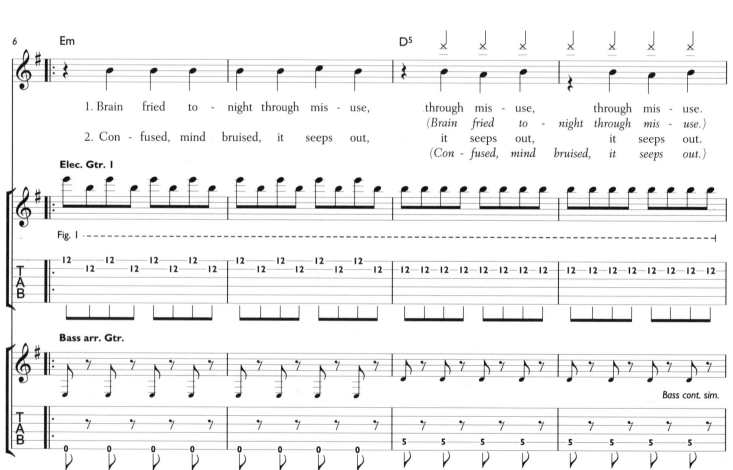

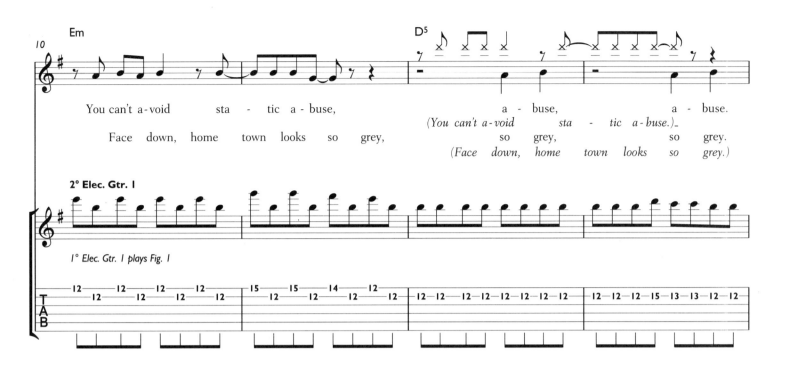

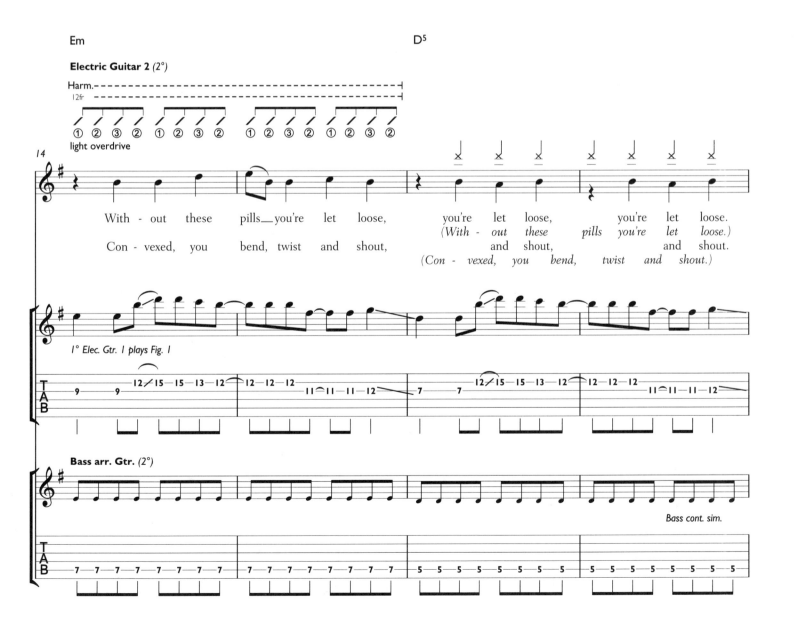

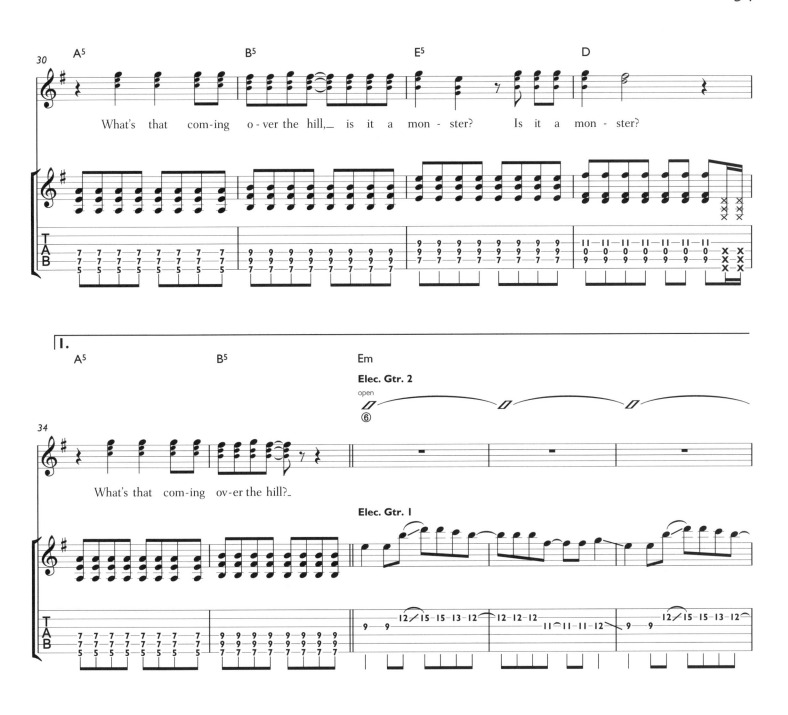

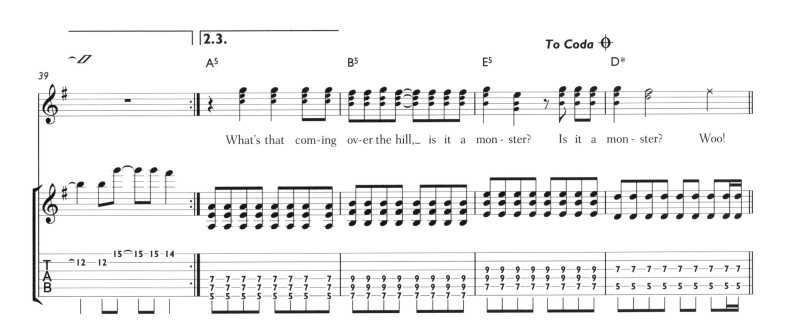

⊕ *Coda*

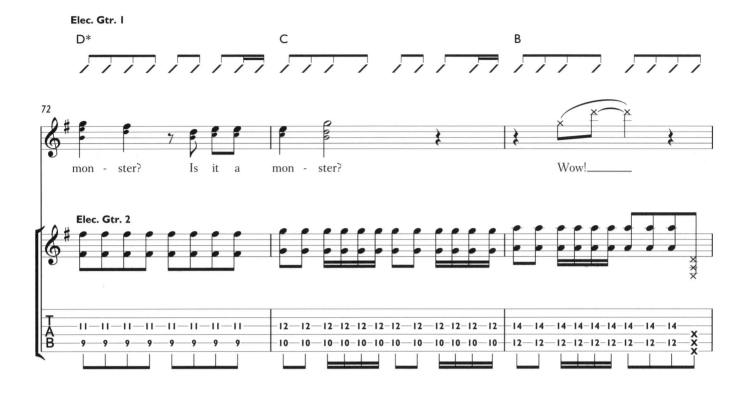

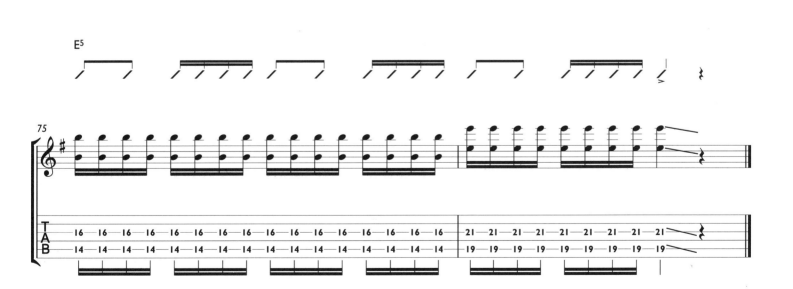

LOST AT HOME

WORDS AND MUSIC BY ROBIN HAWKINS, JAMES FROST, IWAN GRIFFITHS AND ALEXANDER PENNIE

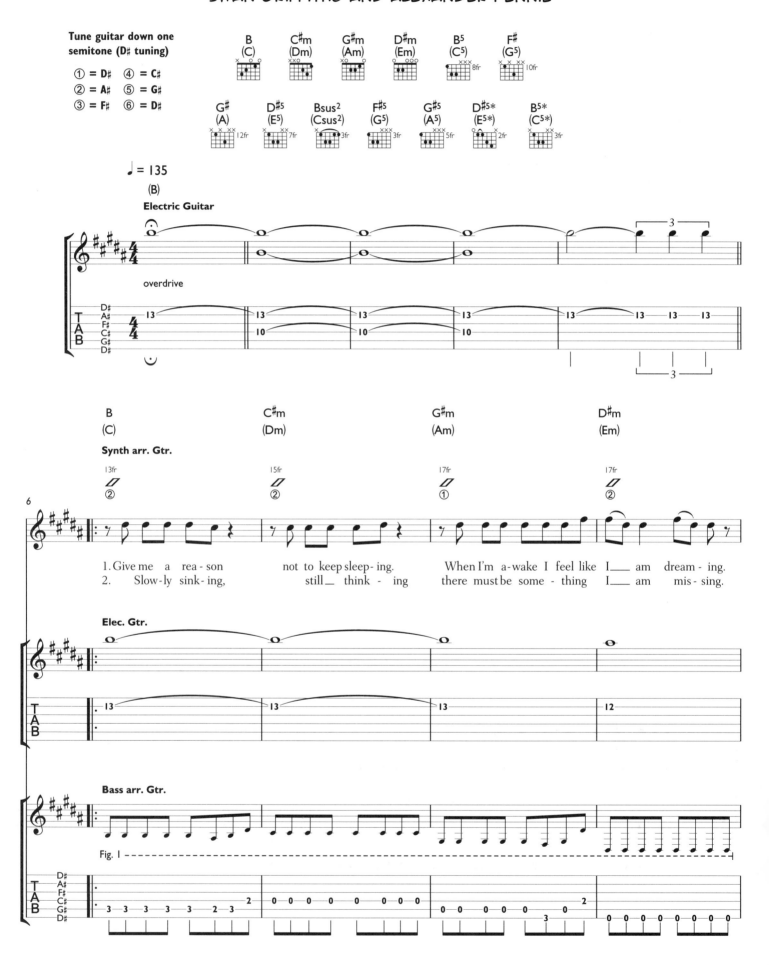

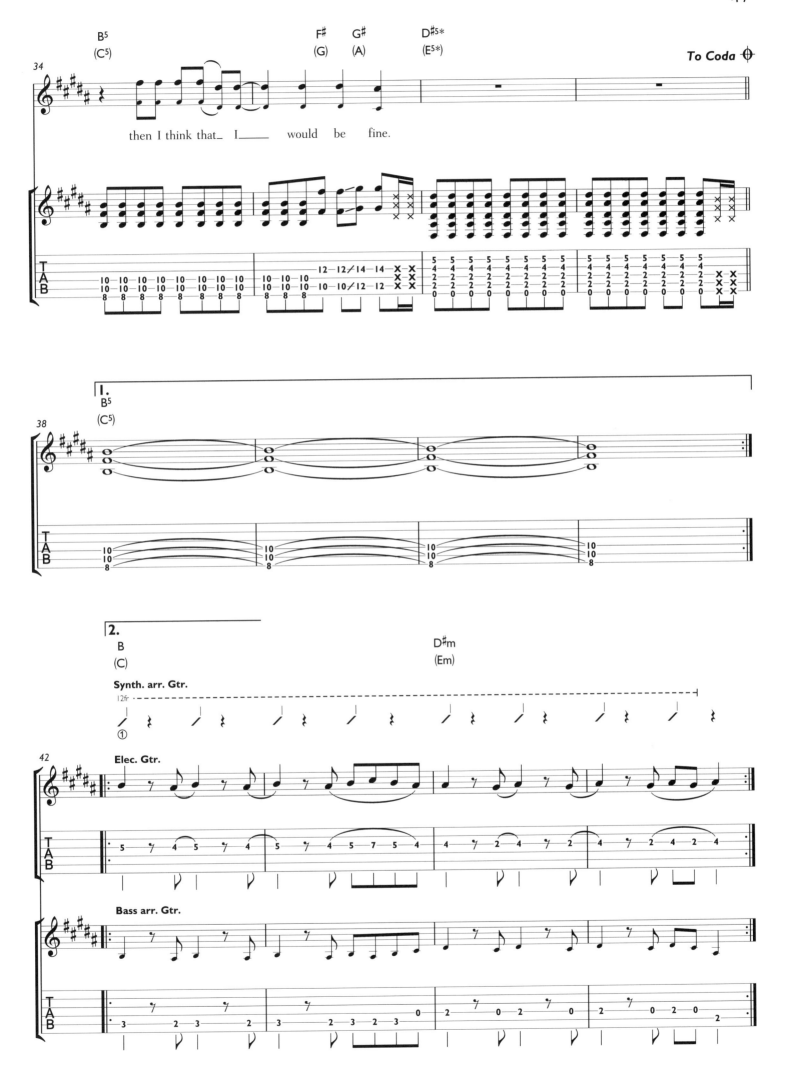

then I think that I would be fine.

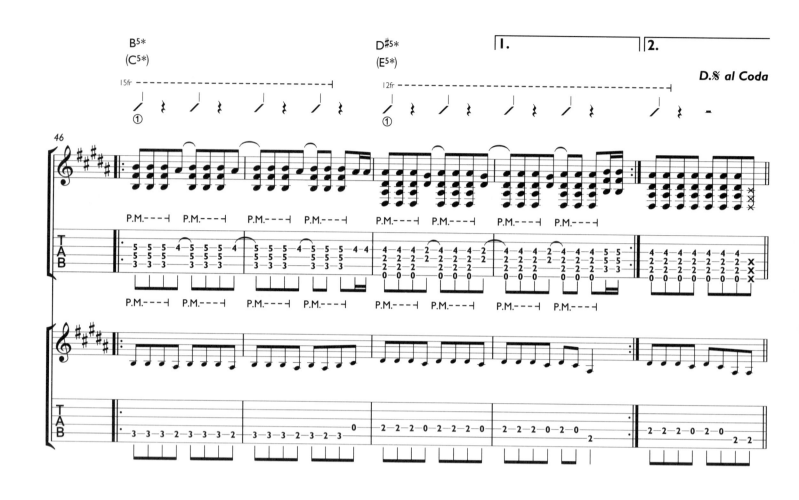

KEEP YOUR EYES PEELED

WORDS AND MUSIC BY ROBIN HAWKINS, JAMES FROST, IWAN GRIFFITHS AND ALEXANDER PENNIE

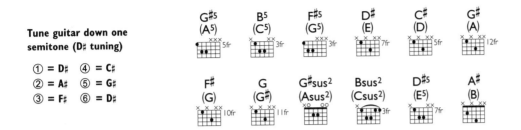

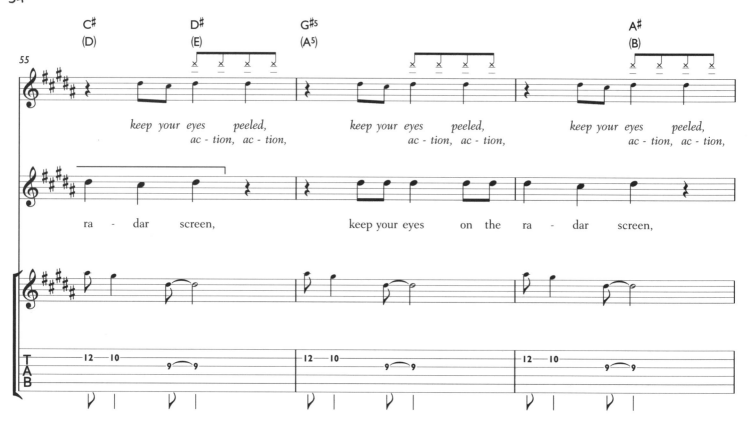

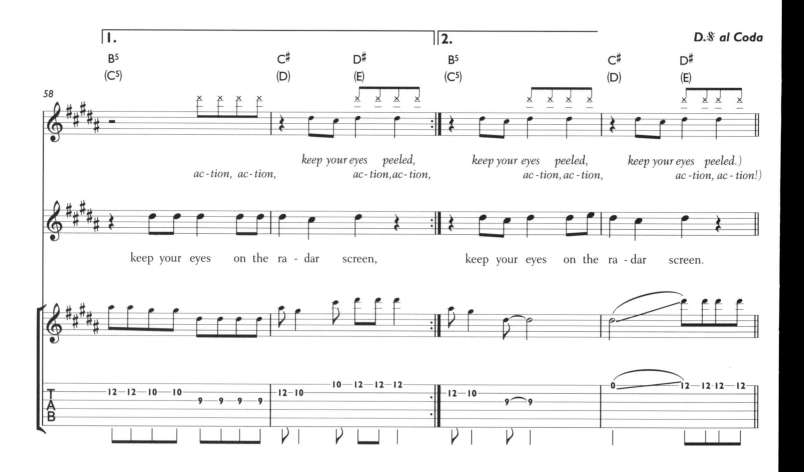

SERIOUSLY... I HATE YOU GUYS

WORDS AND MUSIC BY ROBIN HAWKINS, JAMES FROST, IWAN GRIFFITHS AND ALEXANDER PENNIE

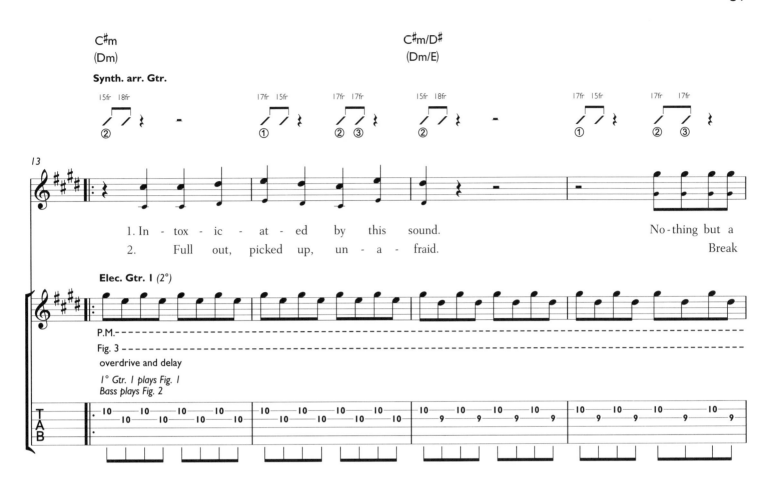

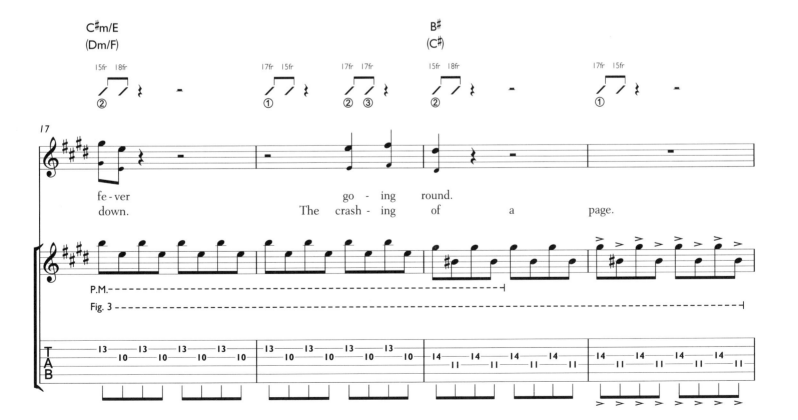

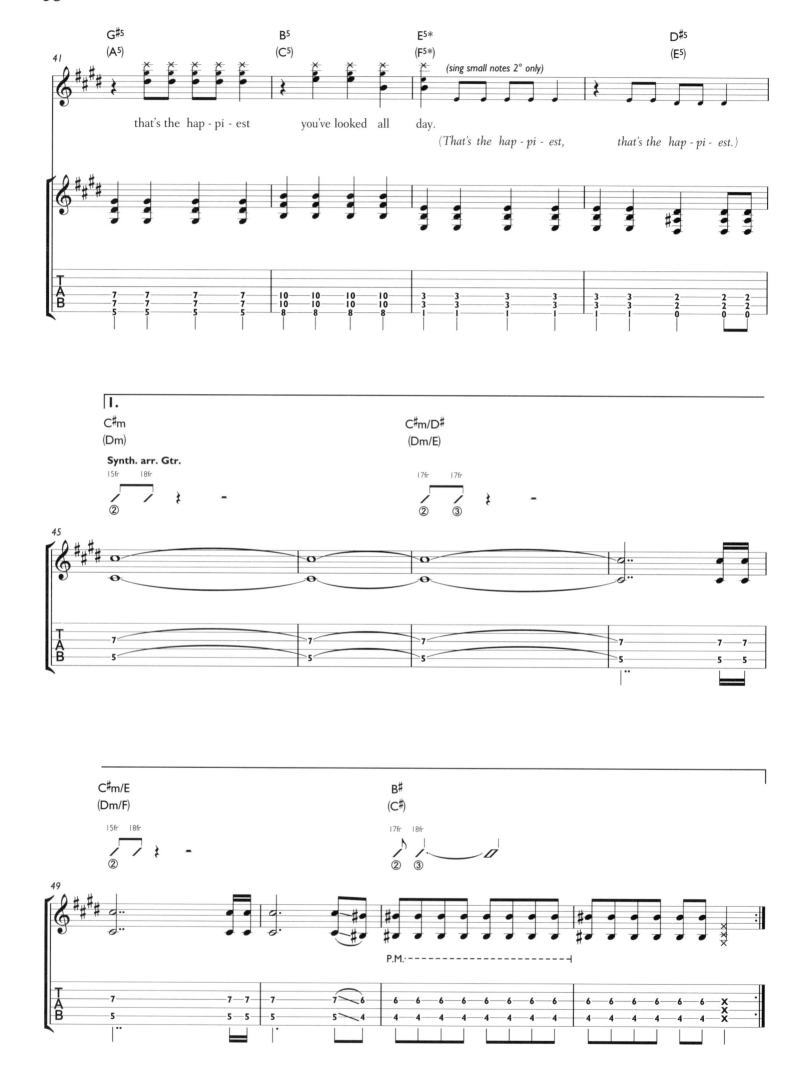

ON THE CAMPAIGN TRAIL

WORDS AND MUSIC BY ROBIN HAWKINS, JAMES FROST, IWAN GRIFFITHS AND ALEXANDER PENNIE

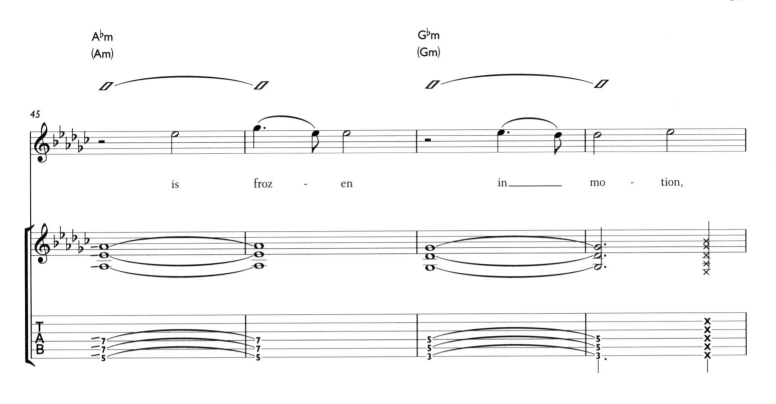

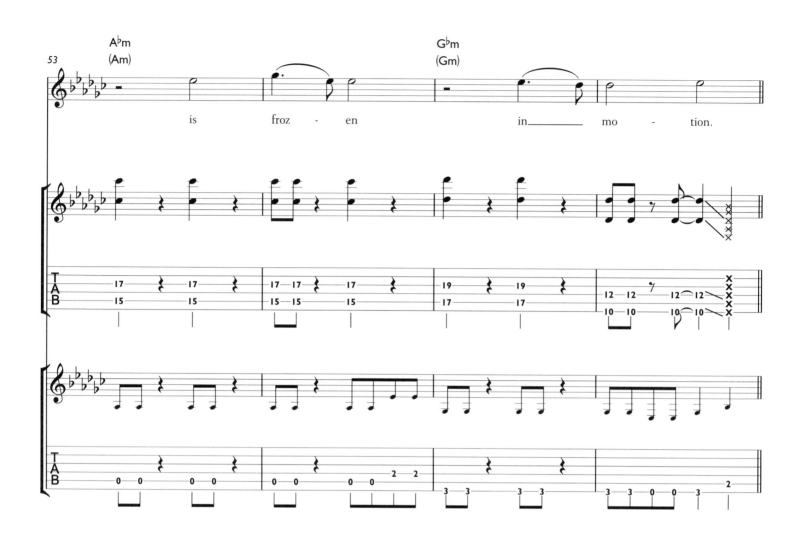

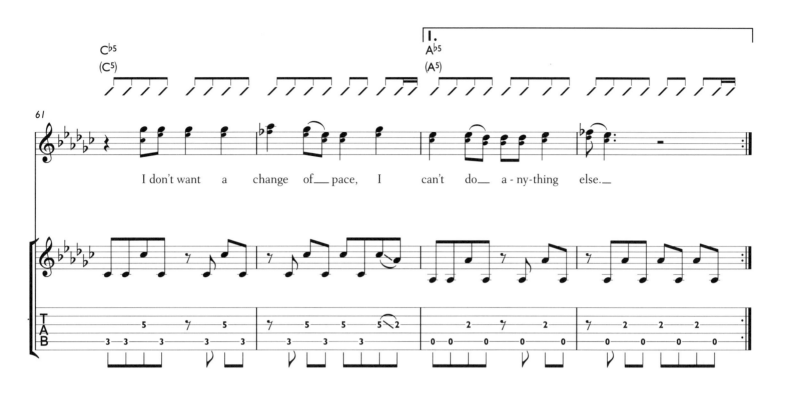

I don't want a change of__ pace, I can't do__ a-ny-thing else.__

(else.) (I can't do__ an-y-thing else.__ I can't do__ an-y-thing else.)

can't do__ an-y-thing else. I can't do__ an-y-thing else. I

TEAM DRAMA

WORDS AND MUSIC BY ROBIN HAWKINS, JAMES FROST, IWAN GRIFFITHS AND ALEXANDER PENNIE

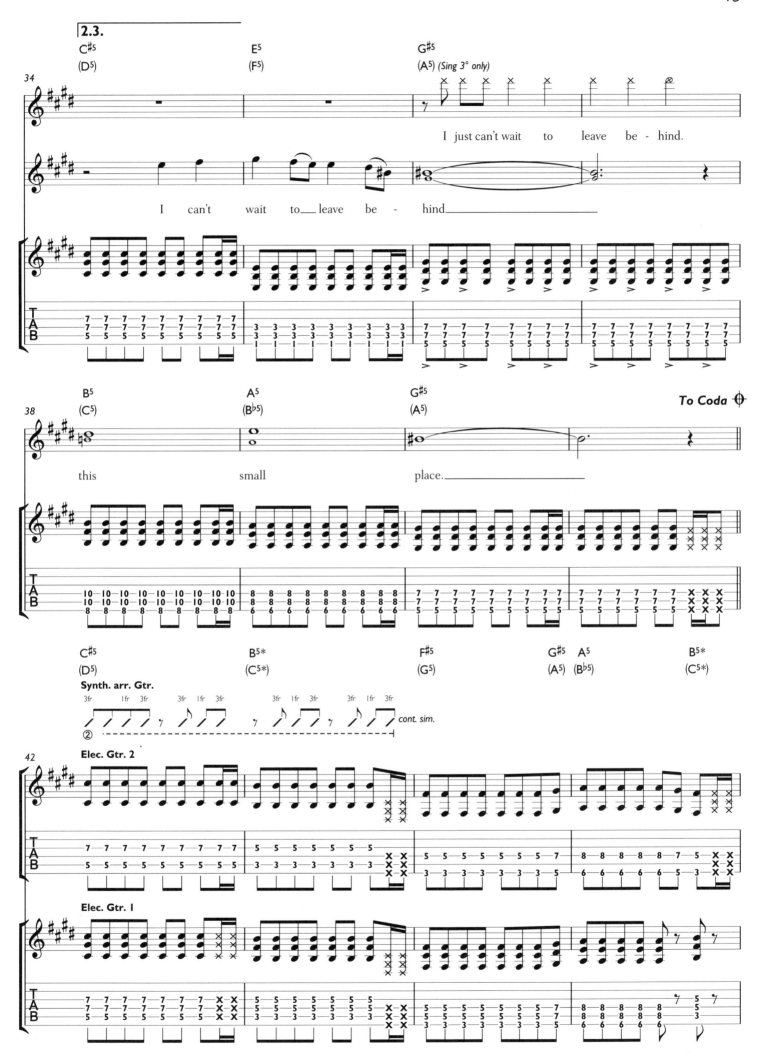

go team, go!

go team, go!

Bass ends

D.𝄋 al Coda

Coda

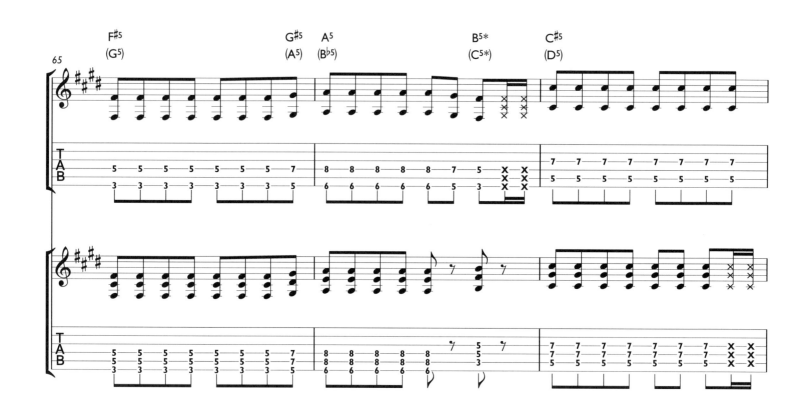

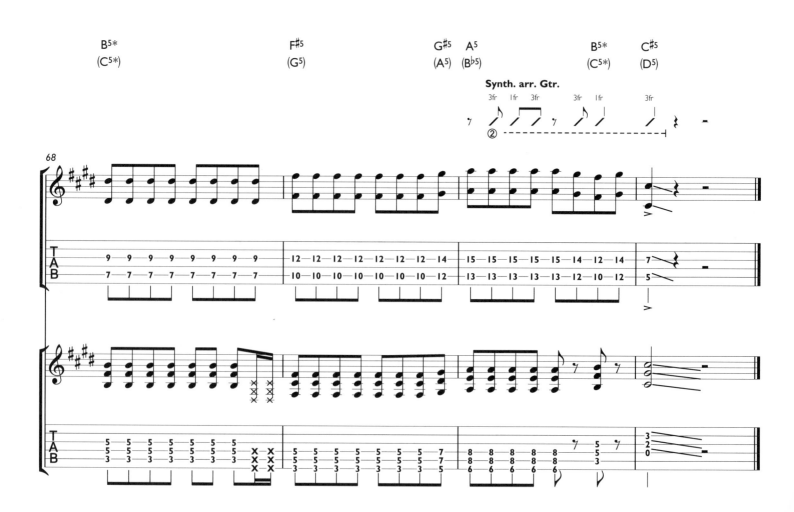

BY MY SIDE

WORDS AND MUSIC BY ROBIN HAWKINS, JAMES FROST, IWAN GRIFFITHS AND ALEXANDER PENNIE

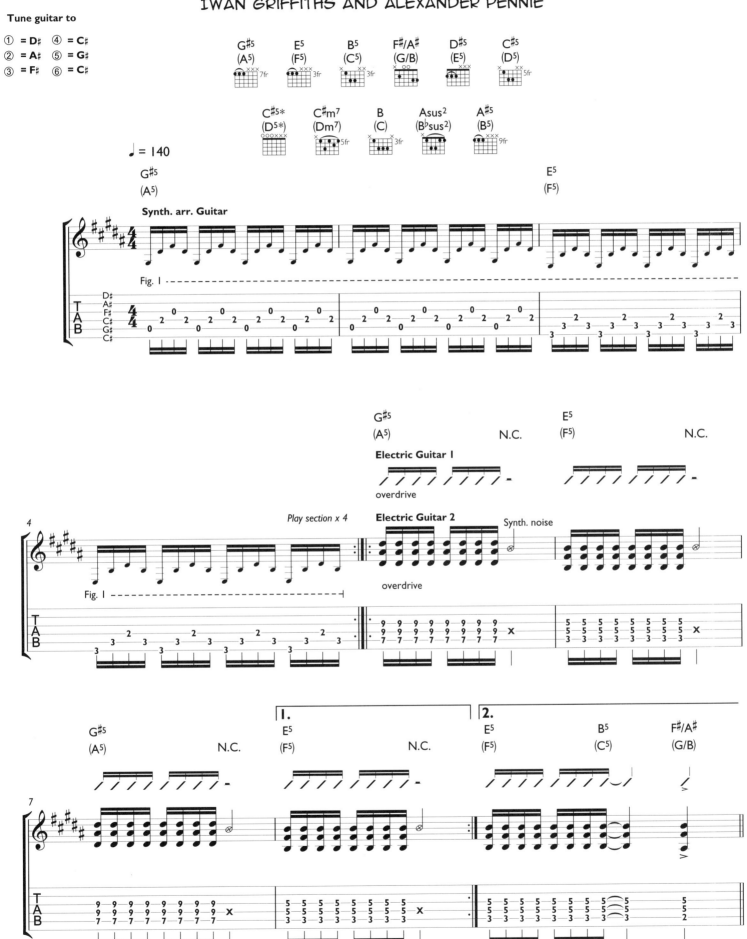

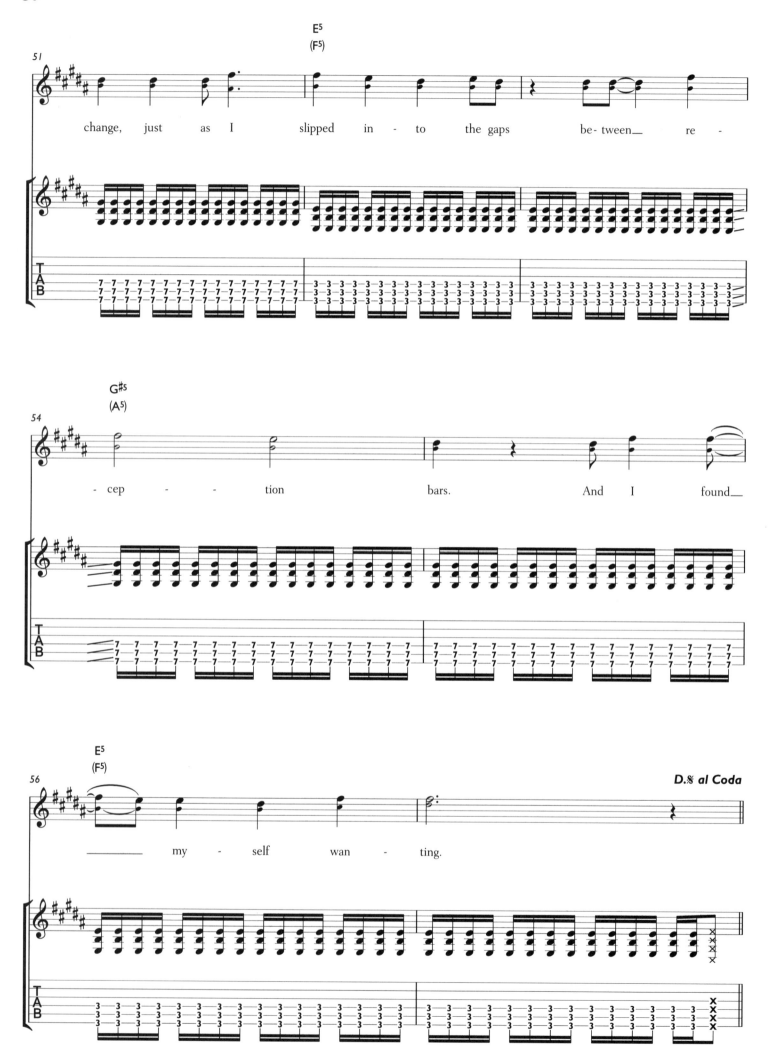

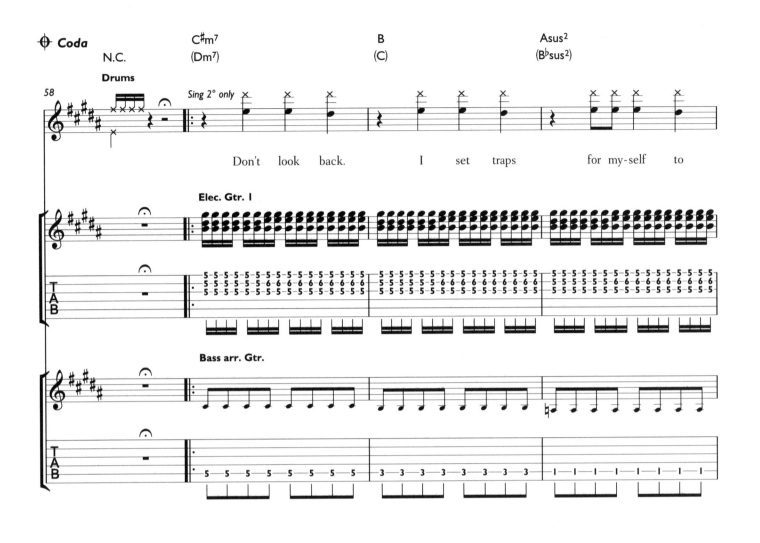

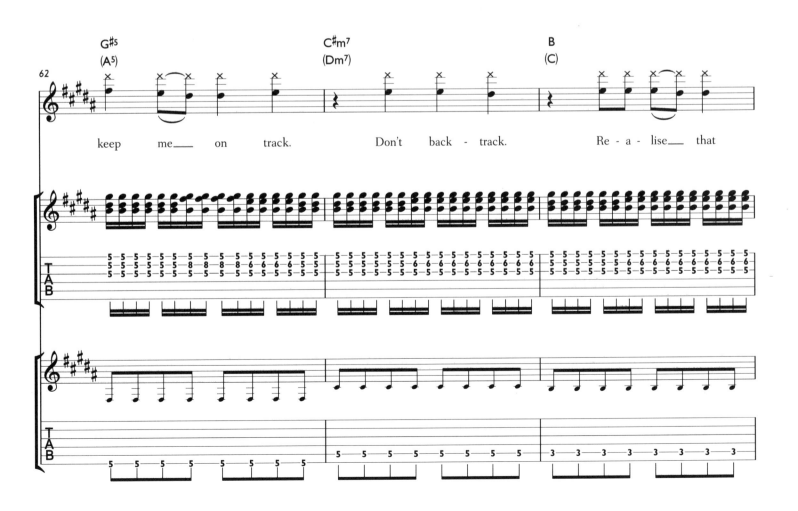

the best de - fense is at - tack.

Is this the end of the world? I can't tell, it's been like this so long.

Is this still you by my side? I can't de - cide if you were here at all.

RATS

WORDS AND MUSIC BY ROBIN HAWKINS, JAMES FROST, IWAN GRIFFITHS AND ALEXANDER PENNIE

a bruise?
- lone.

He's smirk-ing un-der his skin,___ our div-ide is
If ev-'ry-one in the room___ could hear them -

steel but pap-er thin,___ I'm break-ing through.
-selves sing out of tune, then they'd feel like I do.

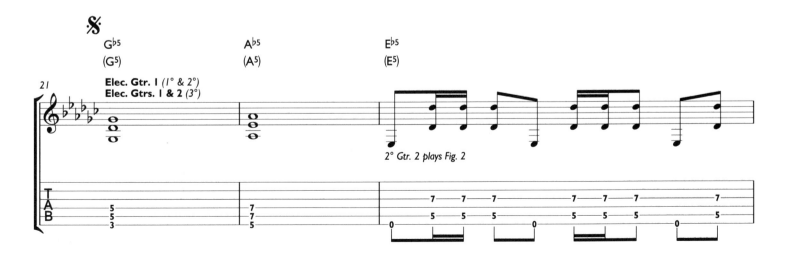

G^{b5} A^{b5} E^{b5}
(G^5) (A^5) (E^5)

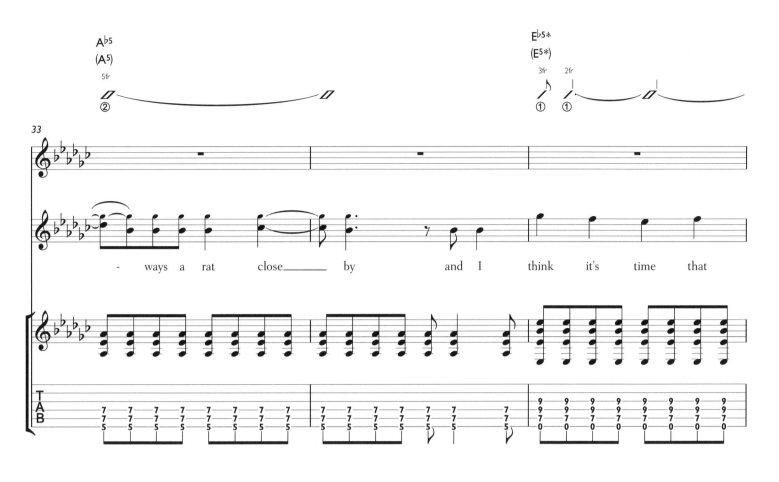

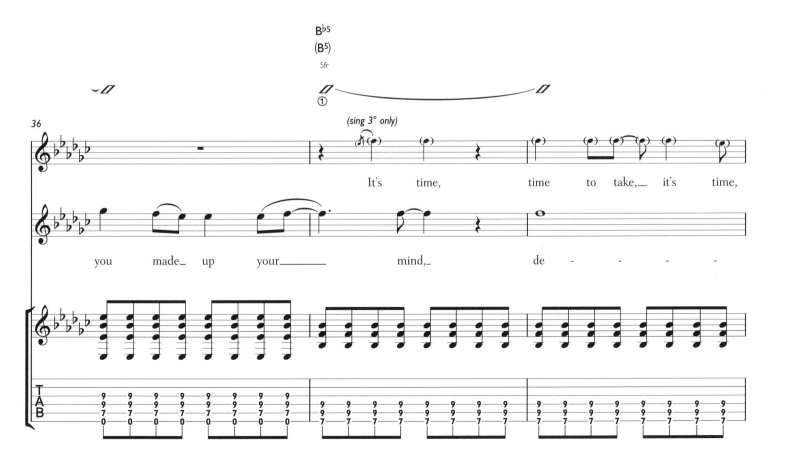

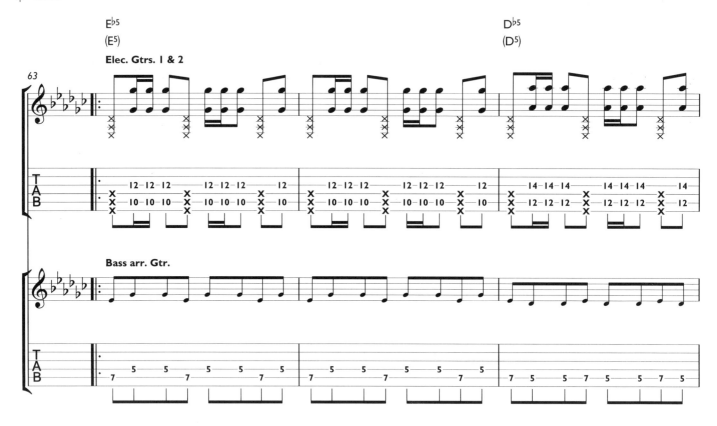

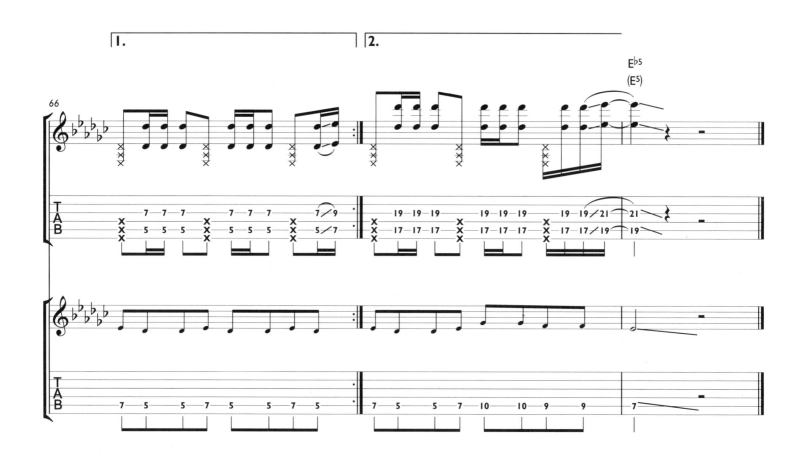